WHAT PEOPLE ARE SAYING ABOUT
THIS ADVENTURE CALLED LIFE . . .

"*This Adventure Called Life* reminds us that change is possible for everyone. It's too easy to accept that the status quo is the best it will ever be. That simply isn't true. If you've had a nagging feeling about changing something in your life, this book will help you make the change *before* you have to rather than *because* you have to."

—Jon Gordon

BEST-SELLING AUTHOR OF *THE ENERGY BUS* AND *THE SEED*

"Most of my career has been focused on helping leaders and organizations understand the power of change. In fact, my blog at philcooke.com is called *The Change Revolution* because change is happening so fast in today's culture that most people are simply overwhelmed and remain stuck in the past. That's why I'm thrilled with Dr. Kent Ingle's new book. It's an owner's manual for how to navigate today's changing and distracted world. Get your hands on this important book and start being a change agent in your family, your community, or your organization. Trust me—you'll never look at the world in the same way again."

—Phil Cooke

FILMMAKER, MEDIA CONSULTANT, AND AUTHOR OF
JOLT: GET THE JUMP ON A WORLD THAT'S CONSTANTLY CHANGING

"You will either live your life by design or default, and this book will help you find the best and highest design for your life. Kent Ingle makes his message of hope accessible to anyone—no matter where they are their journey. This isn't a book full of Christian vocabulary or insider jargon: it is real talk about real change in a way that makes it relevant to your life right now. This needs to be the next book you read."

—Mark Sanborn
BEST-SELLING AUTHOR OF *THE FRED FACTOR*

"Kent Ingle lives what he writes about. That means you can trust what you read to come from real life experience. So many people have already been encouraged to make significant changes because of Kent Ingle's passion and personal example. This book will help you, too."

—Dr. George O. Wood
GENERAL SUPERINTENDENT OF THE ASSEMBLIES OF GOD, USA

"Kent Ingle is a *leader's* leader! As pastor, college dean, or university president, he has made a positive impact. For decades I have studied leaders. Some 'leaders' don't lead, they just manage. Kent knows how to lead. In this practical book, Kent details proven steps necessary to be an effective leader. *This Adventure Called Life* is a must read for those who want to sharpen their leadership skills and for those who want to be leaders."

—Dr. Don Argue
FORMER PRESIDENT AND CURRENT
CHANCELLOR OF NORTHWEST UNIVERSITY

"This adventure called life isn't fully lived until you discover your Divine design. Kent Ingle has personally shaped my life by helping me take hold of my calling, grasp my true identity, and find my divine design. His life, his leadership, and the many lives he has impacted are evidence to the wisdom found in this book. No matter your age or occupation, you need this book."

—Taylor Wilkerson
SOUTHEASTERN UNIVERSITY ALUMNUS,
STUDENT AT PRINCETON THEOLOGICAL SEMINARY

"It's one thing to know God has a unique purpose for our lives. It's another thing to discover this purpose and actually live it out. Dr. Kent Ingle knows how to guide you in this process unlike anyone else. Through Dr. Ingle's leadership, our church has been honored to partner with Southeastern University in developing the next-generation of servant leaders who are living out their God-given purpose. Students and individuals from all stages of life in our church have benefited from Dr. Ingle's leadership, and I know you will too. Make this the next book you read."

—Stovall Weems
LEAD PASTOR, CELEBRATION CHURCH

THIS ADVENTURE CALLED LIFE

DISCOVERING YOUR DIVINE DESIGN

Kent Ingle

Published by Influence Resources
1445 North Boonville Avenue
Springfield, Missouri 65802

Collaboration and Developmental Editing: Ben Stroup
(www.benstroup.com)—Greenbrier, TN

Cover design by James Gerhold

Interior design by Prodigy Pixel (www.prodigypixel.com)

ISBN: 978-1-93830-913-7
Printed in the United States of America
16 15 14 13 • 1 2 3 4 5

To my grandmother, Zeda Sunderwirth.
You forever etched in my mind, heart, and soul
the declaration of Ephesians 2:10—"You are God's masterpiece."
You taught me to cooperate with the Divine Artist,
accept the unique process of design,
and always appreciate the Master's work.

CONTENTS

1   Foreword

5   Introduction

15   STEP ONE—Catalyst

25   STEP TWO—Reflection

35   STEP THREE—Decision

45   STEP FOUR—Confirmation

55   STEP FIVE—Preparation

65   STEP SIX—Step Out

75   STEP SEVEN—Discover

85   Conclusion

93   Appendix

        Journaling Exercise

        Scripture Guide for Personal Devotion

        Discussion Guide for Groups

        Suggested Reading List

119   About the Author

121   About Southeastern University

FOREWORD

One of the most empowering things we can know about ourselves is that we have purpose, meaning, and significance. To live life without knowing these things, robs us of the joy we are promised. Personal change and transformation are not always easy, fun, or predictable. But we have no other choice but to say yes.

No one understands this better than Dr. Kent Ingle. I can say with confidence that I wish Dr. Ingle had been my president when I was in college. His dedication to students and to be a student of life is inspirational and encouraging.

I know how much time he spends one-on-one mentoring the students who attend Southeastern University. The decision to use his time in this way is costly, but I suspect Dr. Ingle knows whatever he has to give up is worth it. To know you have changed a life forever is the clearest picture of redemption we'll see this side of heaven.

The college years are important. It's a time of great transition where we move from being completely dependent upon our parents to being independent and productive people. The rapid change comes so fast it can be overwhelming. If only I had had a book like this to help make sense of all that I was feeling and experiencing. It wouldn't have made it any easier to endure, but I would have been aware of what was going on around me and in me.

Each person has within a divinely gifted destiny. It is our responsibility to cultivate our skills, assets, and gifts to be activated in God's kingdom in a special and unique way. You are the only you there ever has been or ever will be.

This is your moment. If you can find the courage to say yes to the adventure when the invitation comes, you'll discover a life of abundance and blessing. And armed with the knowledge presented as a process in this book, you'll have all you need to step through each phase of the adventure of your life to discover your divine design.

—**Mark Batterson**
LEAD PASTOR, NATIONAL COMMUNITY CHURCH, WASHINGTON DC
AUTHOR OF *THE CIRCLE MAKER* AND *SOULPRINT*

INTRODUCTION

L ife is a series of decisions. It doesn't simply happen by chance. The details are more clear and specific than random. Life— in short—is a composition of the decisions we make not just today but over a long period of time.

Each person has a unique and specific role in the world. We aren't cosmic robots engineered to execute on command. At times, the tough decisions we face make us wish someone would just take over and decide for us, but a life controlled by someone or something else isn't a life anyone wants to live. We possess the power to create the lives we desire and to define the legacy we leave behind.

Some people live like victims of time commitments and obligations. The phone rings, they answer. The computer chimes, they stop to respond. The next item on their to-do list presses intensely . . . so they work an extra hour.

The Call to Adventure

If life is a series of decisions, then it's also a series of interruptions. Sometimes those interruptions are unexpected human encounters. Sometimes they're unanticipated notices from the electronic devices we carry. But sometimes those interruptions are much more.

Not all interruptions are bad, and not all are intrusive. In fact, some of the most important interruptions we experience in life are so subtle we'll miss them completely if we're not paying attention.

Sometimes interruptions are exactly what we need. They're a call to adventure—an opportunity to experience life in abundance and with greater awareness. It may take us years to realize it, but adventure is the element of life many of us are missing. We desperately want it, but we fear it at the same time.

The Nudge

Adventure comes to us in many forms. It may be a conversation with a casual acquaintance or a close friend. It may be a set of circumstances that point to a moment of decision—whether big or small. It may be the dots that suddenly connect and become a clear indication of what will come next.

Adventure isn't always pleasant. Olympic athletes are filled with pride knowing they will compete for their country on the world's stage, but they also know the training and commitment it takes to get there will be intense, unforgiving, and relentless.

Adventure isn't always predictable. I'm not sure who introduced the strange idea that life could somehow be contained within a formula. Life is much more complex than checking anyone's set of boxes—including our own. There's nothing predictable about life other than what we do with what is right in front of us.

Adventure isn't free of pain and suffering. No writer is free from the effort it takes to put words on a page. No executive is free from hard work and perseverance to strategically lead an organization. No athlete is free from disciplined training and practice. It's in wrestling through the pain and suffering that we uncover the richness hidden within the adventure we've been called to.

The Decision to Accept

We have no one to blame but ourselves. The lives we lead are a direct result of the choices we make. When we receive a call to adventure, it's up to each of us to decide whether to accept or pass on that window of opportunity.

That's not to say we'll receive some sort of cosmic judgment if we fail to take the adventure before us at the moment. There will be another call to adventure . . . because life is full of them. There's no need to stress about getting it right. No one gets it right 100 percent of the time. That would require access to the bigger picture of life, which is clearly beyond our capacity to see or to understand right now.

All we know is what has been and what is now. All we can be sure of is greater things will come. All we can count on is a call to adventure . . . not just once but many times. The decision to accept each call will be made in direct relationship to our awareness of the opportunity at hand.

Destined for Greatness

You were destined for greatness. That doesn't necessarily mean you'll have significant power over masses of people or that you'll have riches untold. That may be the case, no one can be sure, but the greatness I'm talking about is more valuable than power, position, or prestige. Greatness—at least for me—is about living a life of significance and meaning.

You only discover your greatness when you accept the call to adventure. In doing so, new things will happen for you. You'll need to let go of what may be comfortable in preparation for the journey. You'll need to consider new options as you explore new territory. You'll need to take steps forward in faith as you live your divine design.

You are not a formula. You are not pre-fabricated. You are not limited by the expectations your present circumstances or other people place upon you. You are free to become all God created you to be.

There's no catch. There's no secret. But you must be willing to see and experience life in new ways. You must be curious about what you know and what you have yet to learn. There must be restlessness within your soul that points to something new.

Our Responsibility

One of the most significant acts we can do in any given moment is to say yes to the call of adventure. To say yes to discovering our divine design. To say yes to a life of clarity, confidence, and conviction.

If you don't get in the habit of saying yes, you'll miss the adventure that will make you into the person of your dreams. No great accomplishment comes without a great price. And for many people the greatest price that comes from saying yes to adventure is the act of leaving where they are today.

The older you get, the more complicated this becomes. Yet the stakes are not any lower for those who accept the call to adventure at a young age. I'm not necessarily talking about the need to sell everything and move into a cave to meditate for the rest of your life. What I'm talking about will undoubtedly result in life change, but it may be an inner change.

No one can live your life for you: not your parents, your boss, your spouse, or your children. To expect (or allow) them to do so negates your divine design—the things inside you that point to the significance and meaning of your life.

Clarity, Confidence, and Conviction

No one wants to wake up one day and realize they missed every call to adventure that came their way. That would be a nightmare. Instead, we want to look back on our lives and see the twists and turns, the chaos and disruptions, the uncertainty and victory as a beautiful symphony of adventure that leaves us with a sense of awe, wonder, and excitement.

So how can you be sure you don't get it wrong? This question comes up a lot. People say they're open to the call to adventure, yet they fear getting it all wrong—making mistakes and a mess out of their lives. It's as if they're convinced there's only one opportunity, one decision, and one moment that will define their entire lives.

Such thinking is flawed. Life is full of decisions. Yes, that's plural. Accepting the call to adventure doesn't happen once . . . but many times over. The sum total of any life experience can't be bound in a single moment, decision, or opportunity. Getting it right, or wrong, is not based on one decision but a series of decisions.

This is good news. Discovering your divine design isn't about getting it right as much as it is about saying yes to as many adventures as possible. Clarity, confidence, and conviction only come when we courageously accept the call to adventure. It's a paradox, I know. But you'll never find clarity, confidence, and conviction unless your life is in motion. And—as you know—life is always in motion. The question is, what direction is yours moving?

Directional Living

No one has all the right answers in the classroom of life. What's more valuable than having the right answers is learning to ask the right questions. It means we're sufficiently aware of our lives to pay attention to the call to adventure when it comes our way.

If you're honest with yourself, you'll admit that you want more than you have and are right now. There are things you wish to change, hope will work out, or dream will come true. We're all like that.

Are you brave enough to follow the direction your adventure might take you? You won't have all the answers. You won't know what will happen next, and you'll have to come to grips with the fact that it might all fall apart before everything is said and done. Nevertheless, the possibility of discovering your divine design is worth the risk, wouldn't you agree?

Directional living isn't about having the answers; it's about understanding how to make decisions. It's about having an inner blueprint that will guide you through your adventure.

Children and Play Dough

I remember playing with Play Dough as a child. This blob of moldable "dough" comes in a variety of colors. Children take the dough out of the canister and create any number of things, limited only by their imaginations and willingness to get their hands messy.

Sometimes the creation doesn't even come close to resembling what the child describes it to be. Yet that doesn't discourage the child. In fact, it makes him even more persuasive as he tries to help us "see" what he "sees" in the blob of dough. And we smile, because we can't help ourselves. There's something deep within that makes us realize the child is right—yes, that is a terrific gold fish!

In a similar way, life comes to us as a blob of dough, and it's our responsibility to make something out of it. As we get our hands "messy" and make a thousand different decisions, we begin to see what others can't see . . . just yet. Over time, we gain a sense of the divine design built within our lives. We realize we have something special the world has yet to recognize. By continuing to experiment, play, and create, we become even more convinced that purpose, meaning, and significance are ours for the taking.

Children don't worry that they can't read the instructions on the Play Dough canister. They don't know to ask for input about what they should create. They aren't afraid they won't produce what they see in their minds and feel in their hearts. They simply create . . . and in creating, they discover that the process is greater than the outcome. Perhaps we should take our cue from them on this one.

At some point in life our brains switch from functioning with the carefree, creative attitude of children to that of careful, critical adults. We stress because we can't find the "directions," and without them, we might get it wrong. We ask for everyone's input because we desire clarity. As a result, we become a combination of other people's expectations—not the uniquely gifted individuals we are created to be. We let fear keep us from accepting the call to adventure. We become good at saying no instead of yes.

Love the Process

When we're young, it's fairly simple to find meaning in life and to understand our role in the world. Then as we mature we become obsessed with understanding how the pieces of life fit together. In a desperate search for meaning, we stifle the spirit of adventure. Yet there's still some of that first creative instinct within us: we desire meaning more than answers; we desire adventure more than certainty; we desire significance more than precision.

If you're going to live out your divine design and journey through life with clarity, confidence, and conviction, you must learn to love the *process* of life. At its core, life is a process, not a linear connection between two dots. It's a call to adventure and an invitation to explore the world with eyes wide open.

The choice is up to you. Will you stay where you are and accept the discomfort and rumbling within your ordinary life? Or are you ready to step into this great adventure called life and discover God's divine design for directional living? I never imagined my life adventure would take me from being a television sports anchor to a university president. This adventure of discovery will take you beyond your wildest dreams.

I invite you to join me on this journey. I don't have all the answers, but I have outlined a process that will help you discover the divine design for your life no matter where you are on your journey. Great things are ahead for you—greater things than you have ever imagined.

All you have to say is yes.

STEP ONE
CATALYST

An adventure is only an inconvenience rightly considered.
An inconvenience is only an adventure wrongly considered.

G. K. CHESTERTON

L ife happens. Whether we think it happens too quickly or not quickly enough usually depends on our place in the timeline of life. When we're young, life moves too slowly; when we're not so young life moves too quickly. Through it all we laugh, we cry, we celebrate, and we wrestle defeat.

That's life. It's not pretty. It's not clean. It's not neat. But it's the life we are born into and the lifestyles we create by the choices we make. It's the daily humdrum of ordinary life. Yet we experience moments when life has a different feeling. It's hard to describe, but we know it when we stumble into these intersections of time and eternity. We may not grasp the significance of the moment, but that doesn't make it any less important.

It can come through an opportunity we weren't anticipating, a conversation we didn't plan to have, or a decision we didn't know we'd have to make. Whatever it is, and however it comes, something deep within us responds.

We can't quite explain it—the experience may only last for a moment—still we recognize that it has opened a window of invitation, and we have a choice to make: will we accept the risk involved in the adventure or will we retreat to what is familiar and comfortable?

There's a big difference between opportunities we try to create and those that God creates for us. In my life, every major step I've taken has come as a result of divine opportunity rather than something I pursued or attempted to orchestrate.

For example, I was pastoring a church in Chicago, Illinois, when I was first approached with the idea of moving into higher education—a path I had never thought about up to that point. Things were going extremely well at the church I was leading. When I had arrived at the church, it was in desperate need of a turnaround. After years of hard work and determination, things had finally begun to change and the church was growing. We were in a good place. I had no reason to look for another ministry opportunity when I received an unexpected phone call.

> There's a big difference between opportunities we try to create and those that God creates for us.

When I picked up the phone, the person on the other end explained my name had been given to him as a possible candidate for the role of dean of the college of ministry at Northwest University in Washington. The one who had recommended me was on the search committee. He also happened to be part of my doctoral committee and had overseen the completion of that program.

This individual told the committee he knew the person with the gifts, skills, passions, and interests to do what needed to be done at Northwest. The university wanted to turn around their college of ministry. Everything I had done up to that point in my own ministry had been about turning difficult situations into opportunities for growth and expansion, so there was an element of this opportunity that was familiar to me.

As I considered this move, I realized just how much it fit my divine design. Higher education wasn't on my radar screen, yet it seemed like a natural next step. After much consideration and prayer, my wife and I decided to accept the opportunity. We left Chicago and moved northwest to take on this new leadership assignment.

UNRECOGNIZED OPPORTUNITY

These peculiar moments happen to everyone, but not everyone recognizes them for what they are. Many simply see them as passing fragments of a puzzle. Rather than see an opportunity embedded in a possibility, they redirect their attention to the tasks and obligations at hand.

There are several reasons why many choose to just walk away from life's invitations to adventure:

Some people see the world as small instead of large and full of unlimited opportunities. This is especially true for people who have never been challenged to reach for something that includes the risk of failure. It may be safe to avoid challenges, but it also robs us of the chance to discover our divine destiny.

Some people are influenced by their environment. When our hearts want to reach for the impossible, we're told by a parent, a boss, or a spouse that they know what's best for us. We're not encouraged to break from the norm to discover clarity, confidence, and conviction because the other person in the equation believes our pursuit is a direct threat to their sense of security.

Some people are held captive to other peoples' expectations. I've been a sports broadcaster, a pastor, a college dean, and now a university president. At every turn, I had to let go of the vision other people had for my life in order to embrace the opportunity before me. Had I not, I would never have experienced the fullness that life has brought me through these moments of transition.

> I had to let go of the vision other people had for my life in order to embrace the opportunity before me.

When we fail to pay attention to the interruptions in life—to see them as windows of opportunity—we leave part of our destiny on the table, but not forever. I'm not trying to give you a guilt trip. But choosing to pass on the invitation now just means you'll have to wait for the next invitation to say yes. In the meantime, you'll live in the midst of unrecognized opportunity.

LIFE IS ALWAYS ABOUT BECOMING

The first two years of our lives on earth are nothing short of a miracle. The transitions we're able to endure are unbelievable. In just twenty-four months, we learn how to roll over, crawl, walk, run, talk, eat table food, etc. Attempting to do this at any other time in life would stress us to the point of a mental breakdown.

Although we may never experience quite the same intensity of change as we mature in life, we're always becoming something new. Even ordinary moments (when life seems boring, predictable, and void of adventure) prepare us for future opportunities to grow, learn, and develop.

Becoming is a natural result of being made in the image of the divine. We are created beings with the power to create. That doesn't mean we have the keys to the source of physical life. It means we possess the power to say yes, to become more mature in the ways we have been uniquely designed and gifted.

As we live our divine destinies, catalysts provide the opportunity to embrace God's intention for our life, work, and purpose. We don't have the capacity to do this on our own—as if that were even possible. What we do have is the power to recognize the catalyst and to say yes or no to the opportunity for change and growth introduced by the catalyst.

A CATALYST PREPARES US FOR WHAT IS NEXT

Webster's Dictionary defines a catalyst as "an agent that provokes or speeds significant change or action."

The purpose of a catalyst is to interrupt the normal flow of life long enough to allow us to observe ourselves and our beliefs. It provides the opportunity to take inventory of the motivations, passions, and desires that drive us. Never underestimate the power of taking this type of personal inventory, because what we believe influences our decisions, our decisions influence our actions, and our actions shape the extent to which we experience abundant life.

Catalysts mark the beginning of a process. Life may seem like a series of unrelated events, decisions, and circumstances, but nothing could be further from the truth. Life is a series of interconnected webs that find strength from being layered together.

Life is a process. When most people think about processes, they think about a definite beginning, middle, and end—but life isn't linear. It was relatively late in human history that linear thinking developed. Up to that point, people viewed life-events and processes as connected and interdependent. And they were right! The process of life looks more like a circle than a line.

Catalysts awaken us to the higher calling and divine destiny that rests within our lives. You may not think of yourself as a divine gift to the world, but you are. God has placed something special within you. Catalysts provide a jump-start to uncover what that special something is and to determine how you can share it with others.

CATALYSTS CALL US TO LOOK WITHIN

The world we live in is consumed with the thoughts, perceptions, and demands of others. We have social media to monitor, emails to answer, and expectations from bosses, professors, spouses, children, and parents to manage. If we're not careful, we can easily lose sight of who we are on the inside.

You may not think of yourself as a divine gift to the world, but you are.

When we recognize that we aren't fully who we've been created to be just yet, we begin to wonder and question what's missing and what's coming. Those disquieting feelings are exactly what you should expect. They are emotional responses to the discomfort coming from deep within. This discomfort is necessary to push us through the process of change. Otherwise, we would retreat to what is known, comfortable, and obvious.

A catalyst is just the first step in discovering the divine design of your life adventure. It is the place we all begin—again and again and again. The question is, will you choose to see each catalyst for what it is or will you dismiss it because hunches and intuition don't seem relevant to your situation and lifestyle?

REJECTION AND REGRET

If a catalyst comes with an invitation to step out and make changes, do you have the ability to say yes or no? Yes, you absolutely do. The choice is yours to make.

Some people carry a tremendous load of guilt and regret because they have passed on some important opportunities. Someone told them that if they got it wrong, there would be no chance to recover. But that's impossible.

If life is a process, then it must be supported by a system. If life is supported by a system, then it must be ongoing. If life is ongoing, then we'll have not one but an endless number of catalysts moving through our lives and endless opportunities to say yes or no.

> **We reject possibilities when we fear losing what is familiar and known and "safe."**

Just because you reject one opportunity for change, your life is not doomed. Rejection doesn't spell doom, it spells fear. We reject possibilities when we fear losing what is familiar and known and "safe."

The only way to step into clarity, confidence, and conviction is to overlook the temptation to pass on the potential of cataclysmic moments and say yes. Leave behind the fear that is holding you back and reach toward the next step.

In letting go, you will find strength.

In going, you will find endurance.

In doing, you will fulfill your divine destiny.

THE COURAGE TO MOVE FORWARD

Not everyone will walk away from the invitation. Some will say yes. They will find the courage to move forward, and they will move in the direction the process will take them.

If you're wondering what happens throughout this process, you'll discover that as you read this book. As you will find, if you're hoping to fast-forward through the process, you'll discover that the only button on life's remote is "play."

Courage is a characteristic of brave individuals who decide to move forward in pursuit of their dreams, goals, and passions. We celebrate people who act in the strength of their courage because we secretly want to believe that we would do the same thing. The truth is you can do the same thing because you have even more courage than you believe.

You can say yes just as easily as you can say no. As those catalysts come into your life, I want to encourage you to accept the invitation to begin the journey. Be forewarned though, your life will never be the same. It will be a process of self-discovery. You'll complete the process with insight about yourself and others that will shape you and propel you into a life of abundance, satisfaction, and fulfillment—which, I suspect, was the Creator's plan all along.

CHAPTER ONE IN REVIEW

Key Ideas

- Circumstances and experiences create opportunities for us to reflect on life's purpose and meaning.

- Today's experiences are catalysts because they move us closer to embracing our unique design.

- If we aren't looking for direction in our lives, we can easily miss it.

REFLECTION

To thine own self be true.

SHAKESPEARE (HAMLET)

Reflection is a skill that is rarely encouraged or taught in our fast-paced American culture. What time is there to stop, look within, and align our passions and interests with our life's work and divine destiny? There are books to read, meetings to attend, blog posts to publish, presentations to make, and soccer teams to coach. The list is endless.

In our culture, we struggle to find value in intentional acts of contemplation and personal reflection. The pace at which we live is simply too fast to allow for anything less than optimum productivity. We've convinced ourselves that anything less is giving up on the American dream.

The paradox of a life without reflection is that it inhibits our progress on the journey of self-discovery. Without a clear understanding of where we are, what shifts are taking place, and where we might be headed, the likelihood of progress is dim.

When the catalyst comes and the invitation is made, the next step is not action but reflection. We need to take careful assessment of who we are and who we are becoming before we can find the necessary clarity to say yes or no. You could say that reflective assessment is the first challenge in our adventure.

It's the step many try to avoid or pass through as quickly as possible. But there's a sure reward if you're patient enough to take time for personal reflection: you'll discover things about yourself and your personal situation that will inform and guide your decisions wisely as you move through this life process.

WHY REFLECTION?

Life gives each of us the same amount of time in a day. Every human being has twenty-four hours to do with as they please. No matter how productive we are or how much effort we put forth, there is no possible way to get more than twenty-four hours out of a day. The truth is days don't run out of time, people do. That's why I encourage you to be intentional in the design of your day.

Without time, there is no space in life to think deeply about what is important. Time is not an opponent on the battlefield of life. Instead, it is an ally to pace us at every turn. Without time, some would spend their lives too quickly.

I strongly encourage you to find time each day to think about what you would like to accomplish, who you would like to meet, and how you can establish expectations for the day. Then, I encourage you to reflect at the end of each day to see how well you accomplished the things you set out to do.

In a perfect world, we would do this consistently. Since most of us don't do that, the catalysts that come into our lives can serve as reminders to slow down and reflect before we proceed in any particular direction—no matter how confident we are that our next steps are the right next steps.

WHAT IS REFLECTION?

There are two types of reflection. One teaches us to empty our minds. Its end goal is to detach the mind and thoughts from life. The other type of reflection teaches us to engage with what is happening within us and around us. The goal of this reflection is to bring the eternal (the Spirit) and the temporary (life on earth) into harmony. When that happens, clarity emerges. This type of reflection is a tremendous benefit on the journey of personal formation, and it is the one I encourage you to practice.

> **No matter how productive we are or how much effort we put forth, there is no possible way to get more than twenty-four hours out of a day.**

There is nothing wrong with the first type of reflection. In fact, it might help you reacquaint yourself with a sustainable pace to life. But in the context of our conversation about making decisions and shaping a godly life, I think it is more valuable to emphasize the reflection that leads to awareness deep within our beings. So many people try to find their confidence and grounding through a variety of variables rather than resting in the constants the Creator breathed into our first breaths.

HOW TO REFLECT

I often come in contact with people who have never been taught how to reflect. It is not a discipline most people acquire unless they intentionally plan for it. I want to provide a framework for you to reflect on your life and the catalyst that has brought possibilities. Here are some strategic questions to guide your thinking:

- How did the catalyst come about?

- Why do you think it happened now?

- What excites you the most about the potential adventure?

- What do you fear?

- What expectations do you have for yourself if you complete the process?

- List the top three moments of success in your life. What did you learn from each?

- List the top three disappointments in your life. What did you learn from each?

- Who has spoken wisdom into your life at specific moments? What do you remember about that wisdom? How did it change you?

- Who are the most significant people in your life right now? What do you think each person would say if you said yes to the possibility of this catalyst?

- What would be the best outcome if you said yes to the call to adventure?

This is not a restricted set of questions; they are suggestions to help guide your thinking. You might want to turn on your iPad, open your laptop, or even take out a pen and paper and write down your responses. This will help you process your thoughts as you sit and reflect.

The degree of clarity you gain from this step in the process will influence your confidence as you move through the next steps of your life journey. Making critical decisions and taking action without proper time for reflection and clarity is not only dangerous, in the end, it is nonproductive.

CONFIRMATION OF A DIVINE OPPORTUNITY

One of my favorite professors from my undergraduate days at Vanguard University would later become president of Vanguard. He was successful both in the classroom and in leadership within higher education. I continue to hold a great deal of respect and admiration for him to this day.

This same professor had gone to Southeastern University as distinguished professor of social ethics prior to my arrival as the university president. When I discovered this, I was even more excited about moving to Southeastern. I knew he would be a mentor and a friend.

> **Making critical decisions and taking action without proper time for reflection and clarity is not only dangerous, in the end, it is nonproductive.**

Before the installation ceremony, he came to my office with a book from his personal library. It was a book about presidential leadership. He wanted me to read it because it had made a tremendous difference in his life.

He had tucked a congratulatory note inside the book along with something I didn't expect. It was a copy of a paper I had completed for his class during my undergraduate studies. I couldn't believe my eyes. Why on earth had he kept that paper for so long?

He explained that he knew I was destined for a position of significant leadership based on my ability to grasp complex ideas at an early age. He knew even then that if I could decipher what I needed to for that particular assignment, I was uniquely gifted to handle major tasks and responsibilities.

He kept my paper all those years because it had inspired him. He explained that he used my paper as an example for other students until he left the classroom for university leadership. I thought to myself what a wonderful gift he had given to me.

> **When we build reflection into the decision-making process, we find confirmation that the journey we are on is—in fact—divinely inspired and filled with possibility.**

That was a moment of affirmation for me. The things I had been passionate about earlier in my life were coming to fruition in that moment. It confirmed that everything I had worked for in the three decades since writing that paper was right on target. This was a divine moment of clarity.

When we build reflection into the decision-making process we find confirmation that the journey we are on is—in fact— divinely inspired and filled with possibility. Each step in our journey builds upon the other. Reflection removes any lingering doubt that the direction we feel led, the possibility provided by the catalyst, is not due to indigestion or a carefree moment of inspiration but is the next divinely designed step on our life journey.

When we find confirmation through conversations, things we read, activities, and the notes we construct about our life experiences, slender threads begin to appear. Without reflection, we might not see them, but when we do, we can be confident that those slender threads are evidence that our journey is truly divinely inspired.

THE CONSEQUENCE OF A LIFE WITHOUT REFLECTION

I spend a lot of time with college freshman. Some of them adjust better than others, and I suspect I know why. It's easy to identify which ones have been guided primarily by their parents' decisions and which ones have gained a sense of self-knowledge and independence by making their own decisions. Those who have a strong sense of self adjust much faster to college life than others. Parents do their children a huge favor when they let them learn the value of reflection in the decision-making process. This leads to a strong sense of self-knowledge and confidence that will pay dividends throughout their lives.

When someone who is older and wiser makes all the decisions for young people, it may increase their chance of avoiding failure, but it decreases the chance they will be prepared to make their way successfully in life. Because I have three children of my own, I understand the deep desire to provide for their success and to protect them from harm and failure, but we may do them harm by trying to protect them too much.

I'm not suggesting we allow our children to fall off a cliff. I am suggesting that we give young people opportunities to make decisions so they learn how to act with courage, conviction, and clarity in making their own decisions. They know what it means to fail and succeed, to say yes and to say no, to reflect and to act.

If we choose to live our lives without reflection, we will never move beyond this step to the next one. We may try, but we'll quickly bounce backwards only to patiently endure until we open ourselves up to the benefits of reflection. Only then will we have the clarity to move forward in the adventures of life.

CHAPTER TWO IN REVIEW

Key Ideas

- Reflection creates space in our hearts and minds to reflect on our purpose in life.

- Meditation is a way of gaining clarity about what is going on within us and around us.

- Reflection confirms that the journey we are on is—in fact—one that is divinely inspired and filled with possibility.

STEP THREE

DECISION

Keep trying. Stay humble. Trust your instincts.
Most importantly, act. When you come to a fork in
the road, take it.

YOGI BERRA

T he decisions you make create the life you live. You can spend
your life talking about your dreams, or you can choose to
live the divine design that resides within. You are the only
one who can be you, do things the way you do, and act on the
things you know to be true, right, and significant.

My wife, Karen, and I had been trying to get pregnant for a
number of years. We endured all the necessary fertility tests. The
doctors couldn't find any reason why we couldn't get pregnant. It
was a difficult and frustrating process. We even went through a
couple of in vitro fertilization procedures without any success.

One evening we received a call from some friends. They
knew of a child in Romania who was two weeks old and had been
abandoned by his mother. This baby needed parents to love him,
and they wanted to know if we would be interested in adopting
him. We were both open to it and felt like this was a divine

moment for us. We had tried so hard for so long and now this opportunity had come to us.

What was even more special about this opportunity was that Karen is part Romanian. Her grandparents had immigrated to the United States in the early twentieth century. This made the significance of finding a child in the country of her heritage even more meaningful.

We first saw our son, Davis, when he was two weeks old. But it was nearly sixteen months before we were able to complete the adoption process and bring him home. There were lots of ups and downs along the way. Through it all we never gave up. In spite of the seemingly endless, difficult days and unexpected challenges, we remained focused.

If there is one universal thing most people experience at the point of decision, it is fear.

While we were going through the adoption process for Davis, we found our daughter Kaila. We first saw her when she was eight months old. We were actually able to bring her home when she was fifteen months old.

And six months after we brought Kaila home, we received a call explaining that Kaila's mom had given birth to a boy. She had abandoned him as well at the orphanage's hospital. The best-case scenario was that the two siblings would be kept together. We agreed and accepted this new child as our own. Davis is now a freshman at Southeastern, Kaila is a senior in high school, and Paxton is a junior.

Karen and I had every reason to sit and sulk because we couldn't get pregnant. But if we had let ourselves become consumed with the obstacles, we would have missed the great adventure of adopting our wonderful children. We were meant to be parents; it just didn't happen in the traditional way. Nevertheless, it doesn't make us any less parents nor does it make our children any less ours. We are a happy family. Yet none of this could have happened if we had not decided to act and move forward at the right time.

DECISIONS, DECISIONS, DECISIONS

By this point in the process, you have experienced a catalyst of some sort. Something has interrupted the normal flow of your life and caused you to reflect on what you know, who you are, and where you are headed. In the midst of your reflection, you have gained clarity and confidence.

Now you're at the point when it's time to act on what you know to be true. Action is what creates change. It's the substance by which our faith in our future, in ourselves, and in God is fashioned. Stepping forward creates a momentum that helps us overcome any obstacles we face along the way.

If there is one universal thing most people experience at the point of decision, it is fear. We don't want to make the wrong decision. The difficult part is we aren't able to tell if our decision is right or wrong until we look back with hindsight. Yet if we impose an expectation of perfection, we set ourselves up for a life of frustration, worry, and doubt.

I want to propose another way to think about decisions. Rather than think of them as the determining factor of our lives, why not think of them as steps that carry us progressively through the ultimate divine design for each one of us. We shouldn't fear making a wrong decision to the point that it keeps us from making any decision at all. Even if we make a mistake and falter and stumble, we can still get up and move forward.

Redemption is part of God's plan, but it is only experienced when we act on what we know to be true.

We should take comfort in that statement. Every decision we make shapes who we are becoming. When we think of life as a journey and we have clarity that the journey is ours to take, we are free to make the decisions that will shape our particular journey.

I meet so many people—young and old—who are stuck between action and contemplation. They fear the decision they want to make might be flawed in some way. They fear their decision will take them far from their destiny and divine design. If that is possible, then the entire process I propose falls apart. Yet from working through this process in my own life, I know it is a true and accurate reflection of how we are shaped, prepared, and activated to be a solution to a special need in the world.

THE ELEMENTS OF EVERY DECISION

I want to take a moment to dissect how we make decisions. This will help us understand how we choose to move forward in our adventure. It's worth noting that each and every step of the journey comes with the option to opt out. This journey is not imposed on us. For it to shape us, it must be something we choose at every twist and turn.

There are five elements of decision-making I'd like for us to consider. Each one builds upon the other. The summation of these elements is a sound decision grounded in both intellectual and intuitive integrity.

Here are the elements of every decision:

1. *Feel or sense an intersection.* You know you are at an intersection in the journey of life when you have more than one option to choose from. Sometimes

the intersection is obvious. But sometimes the intersection is much more subtle. Whatever your intersection, you know you need to make a decision in order to move forward.

2. *Consider the catalyst that brought you to the intersection.* Think about the catalyst of Step One. What happened that caused you to consider a change? There may be some details that underscore how a particular moment or experience or event or interaction with someone seemed uniquely significant.

3. *Evaluate your options and the implications of each.* Understand your options and evaluate carefully what would happen if you moved in each available direction. Imagine yourself in each situation. Think about the options and the potential results of choosing those options. We can never know the future, but we can imagine how our different decisions might affect the ultimate outcome of our lives.

4. *Write down your next steps.* Once you decide to move in a particular direction, it's important to understand your next steps. Writing these down makes your decision real rather than just an inner debate. This written overview of your next steps will support and guide you while your head catches up with your intuition.

5. *Come to a conclusion.* At some point in the decision-making process, you have to make the call. If you stand at the intersection too long, the options might

change. If you fail to move forward, you'll have to wait for the next intersection. If you choose to move, then you'll continue through the formation process and will be ready to step forward with clarity, confidence, and conviction.

Now that you understand the elements of how to make a decision, can you see how we are formed by our decisions? Contemplating options, considering results, and assuming responsibility for your choice is a multi-disciplinary experience that will never leave you the same, whether you choose to move forward or not. It is impossible to stay the same—no matter what decision you make.

WHY DECISIONS ARE NECESSARY

No one ever comes to the point of decision without a nagging feeling that stepping out into this new adventure could be all wrong. That's simply part of the adventure. If our lives were handed to us completely mapped out, there would be no discovery and no courage in making decisions and moving forward.

If our lives were handed to us completely mapped out, there would be no discovery and no courage in making decisions and moving forward.

Quite frankly, life would be incredibly boring if we never stood at the brink of a decision and wondered what might happen next. The goal is not to eliminate the fear of uncertainty. That's part of what makes us human. It also confirms that the decision we face is an important one.

Some people try to avoid decisions at all cost. That seems a pity, because while decisions may be difficult, they're an exciting confirmation that we're on a journey toward new things. There's nothing more exhilarating than living at the intersection of opportunity and decision. This is when you know you are truly alive and not just drifting through life without purpose, meaning, or significance.

> There's nothing more exhilarating than living at the intersection of opportunity and decision.

Decisions also prove we are committed to live our lives to the full. Making a decision is evidence that we have enough faith in the process, in ourselves, and in our Creator to act. This is all we need to move to the next step.

WARNING—GOOD THINGS WILL HAPPEN

The apostle Paul wrote in Romans 8:28 (NKJV) that, "all things work together for good to those who love God." This is my philosophy. Not only do I disagree with the thinking that we must fear making the wrong decision, I also don't accept the premise that our decisions will prevent us from experiencing good things in life.

Yes, you can make decisions that bring harm to yourself and others. Those decisions can dramatically alter your life. However, I would also add that those experiences can shape you into an instrument of grace for others.

God didn't stop working in our lives at the moment of our birth. He is actively working out His design in our lives through every decision we make, through every step we take. God takes all things—even the "bad" decisions we make and the consequences we face—and works them together for good in our lives. Redemption is real and reminds us that the act of making a decision is not a "sudden death" experience. It's an action that moves us forward.

There's one more thing I want you to know: decisions help us connect the seemingly random events in our lives into a carefully crafted web of transformation that points to the future. Avoiding the moment of decision doesn't count you out but limits your ability to glimpse the big picture of your life journey. You can never know the future . . . but you can anticipate it and relish it. You'll never see the entire map of your journey, but each decision that moves you one step farther along confirms that you are a unique person with special gifts and talents to offer the world.

CHAPTER THREE IN REVIEW

Key Ideas

- Reflection is wasted if it doesn't lead to a moment of decision.

- Decisions are steps that carry us toward God's divine design for each of our lives.

- You can spend your life talking about your dreams, or you can choose to live into the divine design that resides within you.

STEP FOUR
CONFIRMATION

If you want a guarantee, buy a toaster.

CLINT EASTWOOD

Your past has uniquely positioned you for the next step on your journey. Your decision to act begins the confirmation process. Confirmation doesn't eliminate the element of surprise or the risk inherent within adventure. Rather, confirmation affirms that everything you've experienced up to this point has been for a purpose.

Some of the experiences in my own life seem completely disconnected. How does a sports broadcaster on the West Coast end up being the president of a thriving university in central Florida? I can't explain it. At every step on my journey, I thought I had reached the lane I would drive in for the rest of my professional career. But my life has never worked out like that.

The step of confirmation affirms moments of clarity and confusion as well as times of charging forward and retreating in defeat—all part of God's divine design. There is more at work within our lives at any given time than we are aware of or privileged to know. There are no guarantees other than our need for confirmation. This is a constant reminder that God is working out our destiny through each and every detail of our lives.

THE SIGNIFICANCE OF CONFIRMATION

With confirmation you realize that you have the skills to accomplish the thing you are considering. Anytime we move in a new direction or move beyond what is comfortable, it's easy to wonder if we'll know what to do once we take that step forward. As you move through the process, God will confirm His plan for you again and again.

Always be aware of what God is teaching you in the moment—whether an enjoyable moment or a difficult moment.

Part of that personal recognition comes from seeing how each twist and turn in life has equipped you with the skills and knowledge to succeed where your divine destiny is leading you. Part of that recognition points to the network of people around you who are positioned to help you. And part comes from realizing things about yourself that you weren't aware of: undiscovered passions and urgings that make you uniquely suited to do what you do.

Confirmation—at least for me—is the step in the process when I feel momentum building. Up to this point, much of the direction has come from within. This step in the journey introduces external sources that affirm you are moving in the right direction. There's a great deal of energy that comes from realizing you're not alone in the discovery process.

I'll never forget the day my pastor found me in the lobby of the church and wanted to speak with me. I was only fifteen years old at the time, and my family and I were members of a large church in Southern California. Many other people wanted the pastor's attention in that moment, but he sought me out. Needless to say, I paid attention to everything he said.

He told me he had been observing my life. He said, "I've seen gifts, talents, and abilities in your life that lead me to believe you are blessed and gifted in some special ways. You will influence a lot of people and make a significant difference in their lives." I didn't know what to say. He explained he would talk to my parents to see if I could spend one day a week working with him at the church. Of course my parents said yes.

I shadowed my pastor in just about every situation imaginable during that time. I went on hospital visits with him. I watched him prepare his weekly messages. Whatever he did, I was right there alongside him one day each week. It was such a meaningful experience.

One of the most valuable lessons he taught me was this: Always be aware of what God is teaching you in the moment—whether an enjoyable moment or a difficult moment. Regardless of the situations I faced, I never lost sight of my gifts and passions. I believed I was designed to accomplish something specific, and I wanted every experience to teach me, shape me, prepare me, and confirm for me what was next.

CHARACTERISTICS OF CONFIRMATION

Confirmation comes in many forms. Having been through this decision-making process multiple times, I've noted some common characteristics of confirmation. This list isn't exhaustive, but it should provide enough information to help you recognize confirmation on your own journey.

1. *People offer seemingly off-the-cuff comments that are surprisingly relevant to what you feel inside.* Have you ever had a conversation when someone made a comment that provided context for a decision you had been wrestling? I have. I usually stop listening at that point in the conversation in my eagerness to "connect the dots" to my dilemma. This type of insight can come not just through a conversation but through sermons, lectures, speeches, etc. Words have a powerful ability to shape our thinking and to help us create the life we want to live.

2. *You read or watch something that makes you pause and think.* I like to highlight sentences in the books I read. I'm reading more and more digital books these days, but I can still highlight, though in a slightly different way. When I am looking for confirmation, it's amazing to me how I discover it in the most unlikely places. God can speak to us through just about anything in life—even television shows, sports broadcasts, and movies.

3. *You know because you "know."* Sometimes we don't have to look any further than within our own hearts and minds to find confirmation. Certain decisions are just obvious. We know they are the right decision. It's okay to act on confirmation that comes from within because your gift mix, personality, and passions drive the confirmation. I would caution you, however, if your thoughts and

feelings are the only source of confirmation. That can be a scary place. Typically it's best not to rely on one source of confirmation. If you are basing your decision totally on your personal thoughts and feelings, I would encourage you to move back to the reflection stage and spend more time there.

4. *Common sense and natural conclusions.* There is nothing wrong with applying a reasonableness factor to the confirmation process. Living into your divine design doesn't mean you throw out logic and reason. Those are skills and aptitudes that should definitely play a role in the discernment process.

5. *Supernatural experiences.* Many people feel divinely called to what they do, and I am not just referring to pastors and evangelists. Some people have unusual experiences that can't be explained within the confines of human experience; these experiences are spiritual encounters created by the Designer of life. It's hard to explain, but you know what I'm talking about if you've had one. These experiences can be subtle and don't necessarily happen to everyone. But people can find confirmation through experiences that seem out of this world. I wouldn't be too concerned if you haven't experienced anything like this. It doesn't mean there is something wrong with you. For those who do have a supernatural experience, it can be a significant marker on their journey.

The presence of any variety of these five things points to what we need in this part of the journey: assurance we are moving in the right direction. It's important to note that you must put yourself in a position to observe these characteristics. This is why Step Two is so important. The discipline of reflection prepares us to recognize confirmation when it comes.

THE COMFORT OF CONFIRMATION

When we receive confirmation, we should celebrate. It's the first part of our journey where we find external sources of affirmation. I find it amazing just how quickly the details come together after the point of confirmation.

> **Once you've had an experience—good or bad—you can't just forget about it. It has become part of who you are.**

I'm not suggesting life is a cakewalk after this point. Actually, the intensity increases significantly. What I can say with confidence is the comfort that accompanies confirmation is real, empowering, and exciting.

There is no genie in a bottle on this one, though. Sorry. You can't rub a lamp and get three wishes. You must do the work necessary on your part. It is in your pursuit that you will find what you are looking for. That has proven to be true for me time and again.

THE POINT OF NO RETURN

There is one final aspect of this phase. When you receive confirmation, you should know that you are at a point of no return. What do I mean? I mean there is no going back to your previous life.

Most things in life are not unknowable or undoable. Once you've had an experience—good or bad—you can't just forget about it. It has become part of who you are. Once you've found strength and wisdom in the words of another person, you can't brush those words aside. Once your heart jumps because you know what you're considering is right, you will never be the same.

This is no reason to avoid the confirmation process. I encourage you to embrace the process because it will transform you into the person God created you to be.

As the president of a university, I try to meet with every incoming freshman and transfer student multiple times throughout their first year. Many come to college undecided, uncertain, and with a certain lack of confidence. My goal is to help them find the confirmation they need about the direction of their lives—or at least to help them understand that college is a process that will prepare them for what's next. Once that happens, everything changes. I can see it in their eyes, hear it in their words, and watch it in their demeanor. They move with a new cadence and have greater clarity about the future.

Affirming confirmation doesn't mean we have all the answers, but it does mark a moment of change in our journey. With knowledge comes responsibility. With responsibility, comes action. It enables us to move through life in a way that shows the world what the abundant life is all about.

CHAPTER FOUR IN REVIEW

Key Ideas

- The discipline of reflection prepares us to recognize confirmation when it comes.

- Confirmation brings the recognition that life has equipped you with the skills and knowledge to succeed where your divine destiny is leading you.

- The step of confirmation affirms moments of clarity and confusion as well as times of charging forward and retreating—all part of God's divine design.

STEP FIVE
PREPARATION

**The more that you read, the more things you will know.
The more that you learn, the more places you'll go.**

DR. SEUSS

C larity, confidence, and conviction are powerful elements that help us move through life, but they are not enough. The knowledge of what to do next is made complete when we choose to take action today to prepare for the challenges of tomorrow. That's why preparation is an essential element of discovering our divine design.

Preparation is likely the least appealing of these seven steps. I get that. It's not as unexpected as a catalyst, as intriguing as personal reflection, as empowering as decision-making, or as affirming as confirmation. Nevertheless, preparation provides the tools we need to move forward on our life journey.

I want to make a disclaimer here. In this chapter we will talk about preparation, including academic education; however, this is not a covert plan to promote university education—or enrollment at Southeastern University. (Although I can't say I would mind if you pursued both.) An academic education can be helpful in preparing you for what's next, but it's not the only means of preparation.

WHY PREPARATION?

People who are on a journey have a deep restlessness within their souls. They are not satisfied with the way things are. Instead, they are reaching for something that is yet to be. We must always push ourselves to do our very best. I call it the stewardship of life.

I'm not suggesting people on a journey are necessarily unhappy. In fact, the opposite is true. I have yet to meet someone who lives with a sense of purpose and mission who doesn't also have a healthy view of life. Life is exciting when you watch every day unfold to reveal another aspect of the masterpiece God is creating from your life.

> Every experience—good and bad—is part of how you are shaped, molded, and crafted into a force of change in the world.

Preparation helps us gain the skills, disciplines, and perspectives we need to complete the next phase of our journey. Sometimes the situations and complexities you face today are hard to understand or connect to a larger purpose, but nothing happens in life by accident. Every experience—good and bad—is part of how you are shaped, molded, and crafted into a force of change in the world. We must never forget that we are always on a mission.

I can honestly say the most difficult situation I have ever endured was the death of my sister and her husband. Both were youth pastors at a church. They had taken a group of students to a local event and had dropped them off at the church and were on their way home.

Before they turned off the highway, a drunk driver hit them head on and killed them instantly. My sister was my only sibling. It was a terrible tragedy.

I had just come home from the television station after anchoring the 11 p.m. sports segment, when I received the horrible phone call about her unfortunate death. It hurt worse than anything I had experienced up to that point in my life.

That tragedy began a deep process of self-reflection. I began to think about investing in people. Specifically, I wanted to come alongside people and help them grow in their faith. I felt I needed to leave behind my decade-long career in sports broadcasting and begin a new journey in church ministry. It seemed that pastoral ministry would give me an opportunity to make a difference in people's lives. Ironically, so much of what I had done up to that point in life uniquely prepared me for this next step.

TYPES OF PREPARATION

Formal education is one of the most basic types of preparation. It includes primary, secondary, college, graduate, and post-graduate studies. While I would be the first to admit that our national approach to formal education could be improved, there is something to be said for maintaining the integrity of the classical process. The primary objective of a classical approach to education is not so much to teach a skill as to train the student to think critically, to write effectively, and to communicate persuasively.

The world is changing faster than most institutions can adapt. This is a glaring reality that plagues not only the academic community but also the business community. To achieve agility, we must be able to pivot in a variety of directions and adapt quickly to change. This is what formal education has done so well for so long.

Another type of preparation is real-world experience. Nothing can replace the skills, expertise, and perspective gained from achieving results. Even if our efforts result in failure, we can still learn valuable lessons.

The various jobs I've held over the years have provided insight I wouldn't have had otherwise. They have connected me to networks of people I might never have met, and they have opened doors that would not have been accessible to me.

Personal disciplines are a third and important type of preparation. If we don't exhibit good financial management, debt might prevent us from saying yes to an exciting opportunity. If we don't take care of our bodies, poor health might prevent us from completing a transition or taking on a demanding role. If we don't prepare our hearts and minds through spiritual disciplines, we might not understand the significance of the subtle shifts in our lives.

> **Preparation—like the process of discovering your divine design—doesn't have a defined beginning and end. It's perpetual.**

A final type of preparation is mentorship. There was a time in our culture when being an apprentice was the basic means to a career. An apprentice shadowed a professional and learned the knowledge and skills of a trade or profession while gaining on-the-job experience. This type of preparation can't be transferred to a classroom.

A variety of people have mentored me over the years. I'm grateful they took the time to pour themselves into my life. Those mentors made me realize how important it is to invest in others.

Currently I am coming alongside the students at Southeastern University. I want to provide a context for their education that will help them transfer valuable classroom lessons into the professional world and beyond.

A LIFE OF PREPARATION

Preparation—like the process of discovering your divine design—doesn't have a defined beginning and end. It's perpetual. Moving through this phase doesn't mean we take a "time-out" from life until we're ready to jump in again. That would severely undercut the balance of theory and practice needed to prepare us for what's ahead.

When I graduated from high school, I had a good sense of the things I was passionate about. I loved communication, and I loved investing in people. However, I had no idea how this would play out in my life.

I decided to attend the local community college to get some general education courses out of way and to save money. I hoped to find clarity about what university I should attend and what major I should pursue.

While at the community college, I took a speech course. After my first speech in front of the class, the professor asked me to meet in her office. She said I had done a great job on the speech, and she believed I had a gift for public speaking. She wanted to help me get exposure in the communications field to see if I might be interested in making a career out of it. I was—of course—open to her suggestions.

She told me about an internship opportunity at a local television station. It was an easy decision in my mind. This particular station was the local NBC affiliate for Bakersfield, California.

I interned directly with the lead sports broadcaster. I helped him write scripts, capture video, edit, and prepare for each broadcast. He taught me everything I needed to know to be a sports anchor.

About three months into the internship, that gentleman was offered and accepted another job. His position was suddenly vacant, and I saw an opportunity. I immediately went to the news director's office and asked for chance to take the job. I explained that I knew everything I needed to know to do the work.

He gave me an opportunity to produce a segment and deliver it on camera. It wasn't live television, but it was as close to being live as it gets. He observed the entire segment and hired me on the spot. That began my ten-year career in sports broadcasting. My preparation had positioned me for that opportunity.

When I started to work in broadcasting, I was very young. In fact, I was eighteen when I became a television anchor, and I didn't have much experience. To tell the truth, I had a lot of rough edges, but I was willing to learn, to do just about anything, and to try everything at least once. I absorbed as much as I could from interactions with a wide variety of people. This positioned me to make my next move.

When I transitioned into ministry, I needed more knowledge in things like theology, church history, and biblical studies. So I went back to college to pursue a formal education in these areas. This would prepare me to lead a congregation of any size.

My preparation to leave local church ministry and move into academia looked different once again. I remember seeking out various university presidents to spend time with them, to learn from them, and to use what I learned from them to shape my ideas and vision. I have learned the value of mentoring others because people have mentored me. That's why, even today, I use a group of people to mentor me—to advise me and guide me through the twists and turns of life.

As you can tell from my story, preparation is not limited to what happens inside the four walls of a classroom, a home, or even an office. It's a combination of various factors that provides a cumulative effect unique to our individual design.

THE PAIN OF PREPARATION

There's something you need to know, if you haven't already picked up on it: every phase of the decision-making process requires that we leave something behind. Our minds are powerful instruments that can cloud the way we see the world around us. They filter out what we don't want to see, hear, or believe.

This often functions as a coping mechanism to various stress points. And make no mistake about it: change is stressful. The preparation phase will reveal what we must leave behind before we can continue on our journey.

Some may need to leave behind faulty assumptions about other people, ways of living, or even ideas about what's possible. We tend to gravitate toward what is familiar and known. This is heavily influenced by how and where we grew up. Sometimes our assumptions about people and situations hold us back from possibilities we can't see.

> **Every phase of the decision-making process requires that we leave something behind.**

Some may need to leave behind the sting of failure. We aren't very old when we learn that a red-hot iron will burn our hands if we touch it. The same is true in life. It's possible to reach out and touch a red-hot iron without necessarily knowing it.

That burn can leave deep scars that prevent us moving forward in our journey.

Some may need to leave behind the glory of success. It's amazing to watch leaders walk away from successful situations to pursue new opportunities. Why would anyone do that? Perhaps because they understand that to rest in the success of today is to place their hope and faith in a period of time and set of circumstances that is changing. Our security comes from remaining actively engaged is the process that is shaping us today.

There is no part of preparation that doesn't ask us to leave something behind in order to take up something new. It can be an idea, an assumption, a skill, or a perspective. If we want to grow, we must break free from what is today so we can embrace a new way of thinking.

Preparation is the glue that will keep you grounded through the chaos of change. It will also keep you from losing sight of who God designed you to be. You are a specific solution to a unique problem in the world. Moving through the preparation phase ensures you are ready to live in your divine destiny.

CHAPTER FIVE IN REVIEW

Key Ideas

- You are presently engaged in preparation for life's journey.

- Every day is an opportunity to learn more about God, your life, and the specific problem in the world you are uniquely designed to solve.

- Preparation is the glue that will keep you grounded through the chaos of change.

STEP SIX
STEP OUT

We must not cease from exploration. And the end of all our exploring will be to arrive where we began and to know the place for the first time.

T. S. ELLIOT

People talk a lot about faith, but few understand the substance of faith. Faith is not something we simply talk about, it's something we work out through the decisions we make and the actions we take.

Faith emerges when you come to a fork in the road. The way ahead feels different, new, and unknown. There is a sense of danger and excitement. Everything up to this point has prepared you to make measurable changes in your life.

It's good that you have followed through each step up to this point. Now you are ready to make a change in your life. It might be resigning from your current job. It might mean selling your beloved dream home. It might mean moving to a different country and starting all over.

Every fork in the road brings a decision. This is truth-telling time. Those who are working through the process will feel the intensity of the moment. The call to adventure and the path to our divine design point us in a certain direction. We must move, or we won't activate that part of our lives.

TRANSITION BEGINS THE TRANSFORMATION PROCESS

When I became president of Southeastern University, I knew I was stepping into an entirely different culture. I had grown up and lived my entire life on the West Coast. California was my home. If you've ever spent time there, you know it is a unique environment. You won't find places like the Sierra Nevada Mountains or Venice Beach anywhere else in the world.

But Southeastern isn't on the West Coast. No, it's on the opposite side of the country. I knew I was in a different place from the moment I arrived. Experiencing something different always creates a certain degree of anxiety. There are new customs, new pronunciations, and new traditions.

Every transition requires three things: faith, courage, and conviction.

I also knew that by stepping into this role at Southeastern I was following a giant personality who had achieved significant things for the school. The former president was extremely successful, well-liked, and respected. To be honest, it was a little intimidating. It's never easy for a leader to follow someone like my predecessor. I would have to cut my own path, but I would also have to work through the established expectations of others.

This transition also came with a great deal of confirmation. Walking into my office for the first time, I could see how all the dots in my life had connected and prepared me for this new role. But it would never have happened if I hadn't stepped out to accept this opportunity—one I hadn't been looking for but one it would have been a mistake not to consider.

LINGERING DOUBTS AND THE POSSIBILITY OF FAILURE

No transition comes without lingering doubts and the possibility of failure. This is all part of the transition process, which can be overwhelming but will result in good things.

If you've ever been around someone who has overcome an addiction, they refer to a basic step in the rehabilitation process with the phrase: "You have to fake it until you make it." What they mean is they have to act first and their feelings will follow. The first time I heard that phrase I dismissed the principle completely. I didn't believe people could fake their way into feeling something. As I have endured more and more change in my life, I have discovered that sometimes we must begin the transition process before our emotions match our assurance about the confirmation.

I have come to respect that phrase as an important part of how life moves us toward new things. Every transition requires three things: faith, courage, and conviction. The other side of these three things are equally powerful: doubt, uncertainty, and fear. The action we take moves us in the direction of one or the other.

STUCK AND NOWHERE TO GO

Have you ever felt stuck? It's a terrible feeling. There is no movement, yet there is a lot of emotion.

Being stuck is a lot like driving a car with a standard transmission. If you have your foot on the gas and the clutch, it doesn't matter how much power you have under the hood, you're not going anywhere. In fact, all you'll do is create a lot of smoke and distraction.

Moving through the process and stopping at this point is a lot like having your foot on the gas and the clutch at the same time. There are exciting things ahead for you, and you have been prepared for this moment, but you have to take the next step. No one can do that for you. You have to muster the courage—in spite of conflicting emotions—to act.

NEVER ALONE

If you've ever tried to navigate your way through a new city or even a different country, it can be completely frustrating. Listening to the voice on your GPS, looking for road signs, avoiding a collision with other vehicles, and arriving at your destination on time can be exhausting. The best-case scenario would be to travel with someone who can guide you along your journey.

> God has big plans for you, and He has given you the Holy Spirit as a guide who resides within you.

God has big plans for you, and He has given you the Holy Spirit as a guide who resides within you. The action you need to take may lead you in a new direction, but it will never take you to a place where you are completely alone. The Holy Spirit is there to guide you.

Every step we take reveals one more piece of the adventure that is ours to experience and help create. Think about children who are learning to walk. They have to decide to take a step. Their parents give them room to try, fall, and get up again, but will never give them so much room that they harm themselves.

The same is true about the Creator. He gives you the space you need to learn to walk, taking one step at a time. And once you learn to walk, He'll expand that space until one day you will learn to run. The process of learning and growing and improving may not always be comfortable, but it will always be exciting.

ASSESSING RISK

Risk is an essential component of growth and progress on the journey of life. Athletes never get better, faster, or stronger without taking the risk to push beyond what they thought possible. A business professional can't advance with increased responsibility without taking a risk and achieving a financial reward. The same is true for you. You will never move toward your divine design without encountering and embracing elements of risk.

Risk is not all bad. It allows us to gauge the probability of success and what the potential payoff might be. It also accounts for the potential for loss.

There are few guarantees in life. The irony perhaps is that one of the certainties of life is that there will be risk. The Creator doesn't give everyone the same appetite for risk. That's a good thing because diversity of personality and drive creates balance. If everyone wanted to start a revolution, no one would be willing to turn that revolution into a new normal. In the same way, if everyone wanted to manage what existed, there would be no change.

JUMPING OFF TO SAVE YOUR LIFE

I want to stress again that I never sought out or intentionally pursued any of the transitions that have become part of my journey. All of them came to me through conversations, circumstances, and personal reflection. I could never have connected the different segments of my life in the way God did.

> **The only way you can continue to grow is to take that next step on the journey of life.**

This was true even in my transition from college dean to university president. Southeastern University had been without a president for two years. They were looking for a leader to turn things around. A search firm hired by the university first reached out to me. Again, I was content in my position as dean at Northwest University. Things were going well, and there was no reason for me to pursue other opportunities.

As I considered the position offered to me at Southeastern University some familiar things began to line up. The opportunity to influence people, to provide leadership in another turnaround situation, and to transform an entire community all appealed to my divine design. Every detail seemed to fit my profile. It was as if this position had been created for me. And my preparation up this point had uniquely prepared me and gifted me for such an opportunity.

For me, every experience in the journey of life seems to create new experiences. When I act in faith and step out into the unknown, then things become clear. Every step I have taken has propelled me toward the next change and the next opportunity. At each step it felt like the intensity of the opportunities and experiences grew as well.

This is the paradox. The only way you can continue to grow is to take that next step on the journey of life. If you walk away from the change that has been confirmed for you, you won't be happy. You'll feel a lingering restlessness that will continually bring you back to this point of transition.

If you don't take the next step on your journey, you'll miss out on the adventure designed for you: a life of fullness, abundance, and blessing. You'll always be longing for what you have missed. Not stepping out doesn't make you a bad person. I want to be clear about that. I'm not outlining the path of sainthood. I am, however, providing the transition points that can carry you into a discovery of your divine destiny.

You will experience setbacks along the way. Discouragement will come. But that's when you lean into the process—not away from it. That's when you press harder and move faster. The quicker you get to the other side, the quicker you'll experience the joy of accomplishment and fulfillment.

Trust is relying on a timetable that is already set in motion. Faith is believing it can be done. Along the way, you'll realize that the only way to save your life is to give it away. This principle is perhaps the summary of this entire process. If you want to build a legacy, you must let go and step out into the unknown. Only then will you find your security. Only then will you realize that you were ready to act.

CHAPTER SIX IN REVIEW

Key Ideas

- Faith is not something we talk about; faith is something that we work out through the decisions we make and the actions we take.

- Every adventure involves risk. It is a key component of your health and growth.

- If you want to build a legacy, you must let go and step out into the unknown.

DISCOVER

Dream as if you'll live forever; live as if you'll die today.

JAMES DEAN

P eople who accomplish great things in life don't do so by accident. They live a disciplined life that is focused on their passions, skills, gifts, and divine design. Discovery becomes a key characteristic of their journey as they continually submit themselves to the process of life and transformation again and again.

Discipline of any kind is something many people in modern culture reject. Frank Sinatra summed up most people's take on life when he sang those timeless lyrics, "I did it my way." This is certainly an option we can choose. But those who lead lives full of significance, meaning, and purpose, recognize that discipline is about keeping our lives in harmony with the character, motives, and intentions of the Creator.

We should not run from living the disciplined life. In fact, you have already disciplined yourself to read this book and think about life through the process I have outlined. You have proven that you are capable of leading a disciplined life.

To live a disciplined life, you must have three things:

1. *An awareness that a greater plan is at work.* Life is greater than our corner of the world. There's a bigger picture that we'll never fully comprehend this side of eternity. We don't need to know the whole story. What we need to know is that moments of discovery remind us that God's greater plan is in motion and those moments will guide us in the direction we are meant to go.

2. *A recognition that distractions will come.* Interruptions are a normal part of daily experience. It's easy to go off-course before we even realize it. Just a degree or two off can lead us far from the process designed to reveal our divine destiny. Distractions will come. However, the disciplined life safeguards us from distractions that might prevent us from moving forward in life.

3. *A desire to build a legacy.* Our legacies will not reside in bank accounts or corner offices. Instead, they will be preserved in the stories people tell about us after we have left this world. Those driven to lead a life of significance realize legacies are built and reside in the love we give and the courage with which we live.

When we see life through the lens of these things, we constantly remain in tune with the ebb and flow that exists outside time and space. The purpose of discipline is not to inhibit or prevent us from having fun or experiencing joy. Life may deal you lemons, but that doesn't mean you have to live as though you were biting into one. The purpose of discipline is to ensure we capture those moments that propel us forward into the persons we are and are becoming.

> **Life may deal you lemons, but that doesn't mean you have to live as though you were biting into one.**

THREE DISCIPLINES

Discipline is not a foreign concept to people who achieve great things. The athlete understands that success on the field depends on the consistency, frequency, and intensity of the activity off the field. The singer understands that success on the stage depends on the hours of practice between performances. The business owner understands that success is often achieved in doing the right things in the right way for a long period of time.

There are three types of discipline that help us discover our divine design:

1. *The discipline of missional living.* We must always seek to understand our personal mission. Part of life management is developing our emotional intelligence and our relational intelligence. Together, emotional intelligence and relational intelligence allow us to observe and recognize our personal God-given mission in life.

2. *The discipline of learning.* Learning doesn't just happen within the four walls of a classroom. Our

formal preparation must be balanced with practical, real-world experience. That is where we test our theories and assumptions. What remains will be what we should hold onto. In order to discover new things about ourselves and others, we must steward the context. We should always be asking ourselves how we are growing, learning, and developing into our divine design.

3. *The discipline of discovery.* In order to discover new things we can't become attached to the status quo, because things always change over time. The stronger our attachment to what is familiar, the less likely we'll accept the next catalyst that invites us to change and the great adventure of life transformation. Discovery is a constant balance between letting go of the former things and taking up new things.

When these three disciplines are present in our lives, we have the tools to move toward complete life transformation. They will change our thinking, our approach, and, ultimately, our choices and decisions. If the decisions we make create the lives we live, then the disciplines with which we live determine what we discover about ourselves and our role in the world.

NEW EXPERIENCES

Anything new and unknown can be scary and create emotional stress, even something as simple as buying a new car. We worry that someone will ding the door or accidentally run into the car and damage it. Imagine the stress of moving to a new city, changing careers, or getting married.

But the stress from moments of transition doesn't have to be a negative experience. Stress can impede our progress or it can propel us forward. It depends on how we interpret the function of that stress.

Discovery is stressful, but the stress itself can lead us to discover something new about ourselves. Stress and anxiety are things that force us to lean into the process that is shaping us along our journey. It is when we lean on *ourselves* that stress becomes toxic.

We do few things in life the same way—or even at all—for decades. It is likely the things you do today didn't exist five or ten years ago. And what you will do in five or ten years has yet to be invented or revealed. Apple only introduced the iPhone in 2007. In just a short period of time, the smartphone has become the de facto telephone device that nearly everyone in the world carries.

DESTINED TO DISCOVER NEW THINGS

You are destined to discover new things. Biology teaches us that living things are constantly multiplying. This is the basis of all living things. When we stop growing and multiplying, we start dying.

I'm convinced that some people have said no to the call to adventure and discovery for so long that something inside them has died. It's a devastating place to be, but one where most people

> **Discovery is stressful, but the stress itself can lead us to discover something new about ourselves.**

have found themselves at one point or another. The good news is you don't have to stay there.

The discovery phase is where we learn about ourselves, the people around us, and our God-given mission. New experiences bring with them new understanding, knowledge, and perspective. These are all things that will help us move forward.

Discovery is exciting because you don't know what's around the corner, but your instinct tells you, you are moving in the right direction. Sometimes words fail to capture our experience. This is especially true during this particular phase.

THE END IS THE BEGINNING

As we discover new things, we have the opportunity to process our experiences thoughtfully and carefully to capture the meaning and significance of every moment. Our legacy is not built upon one experience or decision. Rather, it's the cumulative effect of a lifetime of decisions, experiences, and transformation.

Discovery will lead to your next catalyst. It will reveal things you didn't know about yourself. Pay attention to those things. They can be cues about how your life will develop as you move through the decision and transformation process once again.

Our legacy is the cumulative effect of a lifetime of decisions, experiences, and transformation.

What we think is the end of the line is often the beginning. There is no better place to be in life than at the end of what we know to do. That is when we are forced to cling to the slender threads that will guide us toward the light of knowledge, awareness, and action. Those are the assets we need to be able to step through life with clarity, confidence, and conviction.

We never complete the discovery of our divine design. Rather, it is something we always strive for and move toward. You are a unique solution to a specific problem in the world. No one else can be you or accomplish the task given to you. The adventure of life is yours for the taking. Say yes. Consider this your invitation to step into what is next.

CHAPTER SEVEN IN REVIEW

Key Ideas

- We must understand our mission. This happens when we view life thoughtfully, carefully, and prayerfully.

- New experiences are valuable because they evoke things that we might never have discovered otherwise.

- Life is full of significant moments that include valuable life-lessons.

CONCLUSION

It has taken me a lifetime to work out what I have shared with you in this book. You and I are not that different. We may be different ages, at different points in our careers, and even live in different countries, but we both have many of the same needs, desires, hopes, and dreams. Whatever separates us from each other isn't strong enough to eliminate the God-given desire to discover our divine design.

I have yet to meet a person who didn't want to have a life of meaning, significance, and abundance. When I get to the end of my time on this earth, I want to look back and see that I stepped through life with clarity, confidence, and conviction. I always want to embrace the adventure of life, and I suspect you do, too. Otherwise, you wouldn't have read this book.

If you simply read it and move on, I will have failed. My hope is that this book has defined a process that brings context to your personal experience. My goal is to provide the tools you need to begin your own life journey with a sense of anticipation, hope, and expectation.

If you have a hunch you're in a time of transition, keep this book close by—along with a blank notebook to record what's going on around you and in you as you move through this process. Refer back to it again and again when you are unsure about yourself or your next move.

Rites of Passage

Modern American culture doesn't celebrate rites of passage in the way that ancient cultures did. In a prescientific world, stories and experience were the tools for life transitions. The stories you heard, the ones you told, and the ones you created, defined who you were and what role you would play in your community. The stories helped you find meaning, purpose, and significance.

Rites of passage mark experiences that change us forever.

Every step was a new one; life was pulling you into uncharted territory. Rites of passage reminded the people who endured them that what was a new step forward for them was a path that many had taken before them. There was comfort in knowing that others had felt the same way. They had endured, and survived . . . and even thrived.

These rites of passage may seem out of sync with modern culture but that is not true. In fact, we have created our own. Things like turning sixteen, twenty-one, graduating from school, getting married, and having children are all modern rites of passage.

Rites of passage mark experiences that change us forever. I can tell you with certainty that after getting married and having children, you will never be the same. Those things will change you completely—along with a variety of other experiences. Rites of passage are grounded in an understanding that life is a process.

The Big Picture

When we move through a process, it's tempting to become so seduced by the steps involved that we miss the big picture. That would be a terrible mistake. The big picture helps us understand the significance of the process. We don't move through each of the seven steps because they are intrinsically valuable. Instead, we follow this path because it will prepare and position us for the challenges of the future.

If there is one criticism I hear from people outside the academic world, it is that university education doesn't adequately prepare students to be productive members of society, good employees, and contributing citizens. While I'm not willing to accept that premise entirely, I do understand and appreciate where many business and community leaders are coming from.

Academia is a great example of an institution that gets lost in the details and fails to keep the process in balance with the big picture. The purpose of education is to equip students for the challenges they have yet to see, anticipate, or face. The university education should equip the next generation with the skills needed to think critically, act decisively, and create positive change in the world.

The Artist's Masterpiece

I love art. Whether it is modern, contemporary, or classic, I am moved by one individual's ability to capture a moment in time forever. What impresses me even more is how one person can look at a blank, white canvas and see something before it is even there.

The process I've outlined is similar. You and I begin as blank canvases. But we alone do not determine what our canvas will look like in the end. The Divine Artist knows the end result before we do. He applies His paint and brush in sudden strokes and subtle touches. It is not up to us to decide all the events and experiences that will shape the portrait of our lives, but it is up to us to observe and act on what we see, experience, and know.

Transformation is a difficult process. If transformation were the point, life would be a cruel taskmaster that forces us to endure the pain and suffering of change. The good news is that is not the case. Through transformation we are shaped into the divine design God has in mind for us.

Over and Over Again

If transformation is the path to uncovering the essence of our beings, then we must get comfortable with chaos. Change is a normal part of life, and we seem to be experiencing it on an increasingly rapid level in our culture. Few things stay the same for long.

In the same way, the process of change and growth isn't something we go through once but over and over again. The reason is that we aren't the same person after the process that we were before the process. If we are constantly changing, people around us will recognize a difference in our thinking, clarity in our decision-making, and a confidence level that seems unexplainable.

Embrace the unknown. Doing so will create the atmosphere that is ripe for personal transformation. Let go of what is comfortable today. It is the only way you'll have the capacity to reach forward to what is next.

You Matter

You are special. Not just because someone told you so. You are special because you were created to solve a specific problem in the world. It is our job to uncover that task and move toward our divine destiny. We do that by moving through the process of change I've outlined in this book.

You have a purpose. Purpose is more than a personal mission statement or individual goals and objectives. Living with purpose means we understand our lives have meaning and significance beyond the temporary things of this world.

You have a divine destiny. You may think you don't have anything special to give the world, but nothing could be farther from the truth! I'm reminded of that when I sit down with people and hear how they are working through this process. Most people can't even begin to imagine all that God has planned for their lives. But I hope that by moving through this process of change they will have an entirely new attitude of excitement toward life changes.

> **Through transformation we are shaped into the divine design God has in mind for us.**

You need to move. The process of change is a constant in our lives. We are either beginning the process, in the middle of the process, or completing the process. If you're not aware of what's going on around you or within you, break away from your routine and spend some time in personal reflection. We were created to accomplish something. Only action creates change.

You matter. There is only one of you in the world. An artist doesn't duplicate his or her work. Each piece is unique and different. In the same way, you are unique and different. Be proud of that. You matter—just like you are. But the Divine Artist won't leave you like you are today. Remember, He sees the big picture.

Next Steps

In the appendix of this book you will find some tools to help you begin the process of discovering your divine design. The first tool you'll find is a journal exercise. Journaling helps us think carefully about what's going on around us and within us. Find a quiet place and work through the questions. I know you'll be surprised by what you uncover.

The next tool is a collection of Scripture verses that will help you learn more about God and His plans for your life. This isn't an exhaustive list, but it will get you started. As you read through the verses in this book or in the Bible, record the ones that mean the most to you. Note how they apply to what is going on in your life at that moment. This will help you see how your life connects to God's divine design.

When you share your journey with others, they'll be glad to celebrate with you along the way.

The last tool is a series of discussion questions to spur your thinking around these seven steps of discovery. The questions are helpful for either a group or an individual. There are no right or wrong answers. However, the more honestly we answer the questions, the greater clarity we'll have about the transformation taking place around us and within us.

A Note of Encouragement

I would like to encourage you to find someone to discuss with you what you've learned in this book. Telling someone else about the transformation we recognize and experience in our lives is an important part of the discovery process. Others might see things we have overlooked. When you share your journey with others, they'll be glad to celebrate with you along the way.

I want to encourage you to keep pressing on. Life is what you make of it. If you want to step through life with clarity, confidence, and conviction, you'll need to be aware of the process by which our divine destiny is cultivated, curated, and crafted into a beautiful masterpiece.

What you know about life today will change as you move through this process again and again. If you embrace change and recognize what the process looks like, you'll learn to push through the hesitations and hindrances that come along the way. Press on toward the success that is right in front of you.

APPENDIX

Journaling Exercise

STEP ONE—CATALYST

Catalysts are moments God uses to shape and refine us. It's possible to have one or more of these experiences each day.

What catalyst experiences have you had lately?

Since a catalyst is an event that moves or shapes us, what do you think God is moving you toward or shaping you for?

What questions do you have about your direction, purpose, and mission in life?

Write down the toughest questions you are wrestling through right now.

STEP TWO—REFLECTION

We usually use mirrors to see a reflection of ourselves. When it comes to discovering your purpose in life, reflection is an act of meditation.

Describe a time when you sat quietly and listened to your thoughts.

Do you find it difficult or easy to meditate? Explain your response.

What are some of the distractions that make it hard for you to meditate? What can you do to remove those distractions?

What individuals have had an influence on your life? Take some time this week to write notes of thanks and encouragement to them.

STEP THREE—DECISION

A decision that isn't followed by action is nothing more than a good idea. It's important for you to develop an action plan for the decisions you make regarding your mission and purpose in life.

How do you make decisions about your future? List the steps you employ to arrive at a decision.

Think for a moment about a bad decision you made. What process did you use to make that decision? Where did you make your mistake?

What are the criteria you use to determine if a decision is the right one?

Think about an upcoming decision. Use the decision-making strategy in this chapter to work through that decision. How does this plan affect your decision-making abilities?

STEP FOUR—CONFIRMATION

We always want to know if we are doing the right things. We want to do the things that will help us discover our divine destiny, but how can we be sure what those things are?

List some circumstances in which you had a good indication that you were doing exactly what you were designed to do.

How did you know?

List some people you know who live with clarity, confidence, and conviction.

When have you consulted one or more of these people about your direction in life?

What is one thing you are doing right now that requires you to have faith?

STEP FIVE—PREPARATION

It seems that we are always preparing for something. It doesn't matter how young or old we are or how much life we have ahead or behind us. Preparation is a big part of life. The situations and people around you are instrumental in your preparation. In the search for God's guidance, the best resources available are often sitting right beside you.

What do you think you are being prepared to do next?

Identify some people who are doing something similar to what you feel called. What are three questions you'd like to ask those people?

Life has a way of weaving together our life experiences and connecting things that originally seemed disconnected. Describe a time when you connected two things that you thought were independent of each other.

What did you learn through the experience above?

What life experiences have you had that also serve to prepare you for what's ahead of you?

STEP SIX—STEP OUT

Life is an adventure of ups and downs that can take our breath away. Ultimately, it is by experiencing those ups and downs that we find the life we desire, the one we were created to live. With the path clearly identified, there is one thing left to do—start moving.

Moving out in faith can be scary. Describe a time when you did something based solely on your faith.

Why did you take such a bold step? What motivated you?

Do you have that sort of motivation right now? If so, where does it come from? If not, where do you expect to get your motivation?

What are some things that distract you? How can you eliminate those distractions and stay focused?

What are three things you will do differently in the week ahead?

STEP SEVEN—DISCOVER

Your personal mission is simply the awareness that there is a plan, purpose, and reason you exist. This doesn't mean you are more important than others; it means that you are an important part of how the world will be changed and brought in line with God's intentions.

How would you describe your mission?

What is the ultimate outcome of that mission? Will it affect people physically, spiritually, or both?

Can you envision yourself fulfilling that mission? What image do you see?

What are you learning along the way?

NOW WHAT?

You've discovered your passion, identified your mission, listed some people who are beside you and . . . this is where it gets serious: We have to keep moving forward. Now that we understand the process, we have to lean into each step and trust the outcome.

You are a masterpiece. What does that mean to you?

How is your life like art? What are you doing to be the art you were designed to be?

Are you expressing your divine destiny through your life or are you trying to become something or someone else?

What people are you influencing and encouraging in their journeys?

What is the difference between living a full life and an abundant life? Which vision is controlling your activities right now?

Scripture Guide for Personal Devotion

TOPIC	REFERENCE	VERSE
Courage	Joshua 1:2	"Moses my servant is dead. Now then, you and all these people, get ready to cross the Jordan River into the land I am about to give to them—to the Israelites."
	Joshua 1:7	"Be strong and very courageous. Be careful to obey all the law my servant Moses gave you; do not turn from it to the right or to the left, that you may be successful wherever you go."
Fear	Isaiah 41:10	So do not fear, for I am with you; do not be dismayed, for I am your God. I will strengthen you and help you; I will uphold you with my righteous right hand.
	Matthew 10:28	Do not be afraid of those who kill the body but cannot kill the soul. Rather, be afraid of the One who can destroy both soul and body in hell.
	Hebrews 13:6	So we say with confidence, "The Lord is my helper; I will not be afraid. What can mere mortals do to me?"

Gifts	1 Corinthians 12:4–6	There are different kinds of gifts, but the same Spirit distributes them. There are different kinds of service, but the same Lord. There are different kinds of working, but in all of them and in everyone it is the same God at work.
	Romans 11:29	For God's gifts and his call are irrevocable.
	Ephesians 4:11–13	So Christ himself gave the apostles, the prophets, the evangelists, the pastors and teachers, to equip his people for works of service, so that the body of Christ may be built up until we all reach unity in the faith and in the knowledge of the Son of God and become mature, attaining to the whole measure of the fullness of Christ.
Calling	2 Thessalonians 1:11	With this in mind, we constantly pray for you, that our God may make you worthy of his calling, and that by his power he may bring to fruition your every desire for goodness and your every deed prompted by faith.
	Acts 16:9	During the night Paul had a vision of a man of Macedonia standing and begging him, "Come over to Macedonia and help us."
	Ephesians 4:1	As a prisoner for the Lord, then, I urge you to live a life worthy of the calling you have received.

	2 Peter 1:10	Therefore, my brothers and sisters, make every effort to confirm your calling and election. For if you do these things, you will never stumble.
Love Others	Micah 6:8	He has shown you, O mortal, what is good. And what does the LORD require of you? To act justly and to love mercy and to walk humbly with your God.
	Mark 12:29–31	"The most important one," answered Jesus, "is this: 'Hear, O Israel: The LORD our God, the LORD is one. Love the LORD your God with all your heart and with all your soul and with all your mind and with all your strength.' The second is this: 'Love your neighbor as yourself.' There is no commandment greater than these."
Perseverance	Hebrews 12:1–3	Therefore, since we are surrounded by such a great cloud of witnesses, let us throw off everything that hinders and the sin that so easily entangles. And let us run with perseverance the race marked out for us, fixing our eyes on Jesus, the pioneer and perfecter of faith. For the joy set before him he endured the cross, scorning its shame, and sat down at the right hand of the throne of God. Consider him who endured such opposition from sinners, so that you will not grow weary and lose heart.

James 1:4	Let perseverance finish its work so that you may be mature and complete, not lacking anything.	
2 Peter 1:5-7	For this very reason, make every effort to add to your faith goodness; and to goodness, knowledge; and to knowledge, self-control; and to self-control, perseverance; and to perseverance, godliness; and to godliness, mutual affection; and to mutual affection, love.	
Romans 5:2-4	And we boast in the hope of the glory of God. Not only so, but we also glory in our sufferings, because we know that suffering produces perseverance; perseverance, character; and character, hope.	

Discussion Guide for Groups

- Describe how a recent experience affected your perception of your purpose in life.

- If viewed as a catalyst, what might that situation lead to in the future?

- What can you do to improve your awareness of the direction of your life?

- Based on what you know about your life right now, what do you believe is divine destiny?

- Think about your daily schedule. When will be the best time for you to spend time in meditation?

- Who are some people who have influenced your life up to this point?

- Why is it so hard to take the first step in an action plan?

- When are you planning to take step one?

- Describe your decision-making skills. Are you confident you can discern the direction for your life? Why or why not?

- What uniqueness do you bring to the world? What unique contribution would you like to make to the world?

- Name one thing you have done that demonstrates faith. How did your confidence level change following that experience?

- What do you think you are being prepared to accomplish?

- What have you learned about yourself by learning about the process outlined in this book?

- How has your life been stitched together to make something beautiful?

- What risks must you take as you move forward with your plan for life?

- How will you stay focused on your journey? What is your strategy for dealing with distractions?

- What is your life's mission?

- What are you learning through recent new experiences?

- What is one thing you are doing now that you never dreamed you could do?

- What valuable life lessons are you learning through your significant moments?

- How does your vision for life compare to the expectations of others? Which vision is controlling your daily activities?

- How can you move toward the unknown with clarity and confidence?

Suggested Reading

Quitter: Closing the Gap Between Your Day Job & Your Dream Job (Jon Acuff)

Soulprint: Discovering Your Divine Destiny (Mark Batterson)

Wild Goose Chase: Reclaim the Adventure of Pursuing God (Mark Batterson)

The Echo Within: Finding Your True Calling (Robert Benson)

The Practice of Godliness: Godliness Has Value for All Things (Jerry Bridges)

Primal Leadership: Learning to Lead with Emotional Intelligence (Daniel Goleman, Richard Boyatzis, and Annie McKee)

Chazown: Define Your Vision, Pursue Your Passion, Live Your Life on Purpose (Craig Groeschel)

Made to Stick: Why Some Ideas Survive and Others Die (Chip Heath and Dan Heath)

Is God Calling Me?: Answering the Question Every Believer Asks (Jeff Iorg)

Leading Change: Why Transformation Efforts Fail (John P. Kotter)

Seizing Your Divine Moment: Dare to Live a Life of Adventure (Erwin McManus)

No More Dreaded Mondays: Ignite Your Passion—and Other Revolutionary Ways to Discover Your True Calling at Work (Dan Miller)

Let Your Life Speak: Listening for the Voice of Vocation (Parker J. Palmer)

Lincoln on Leadership: Executive Strategies for Tough Times (Donald T. Phillips)

The Purpose Driven Life: What on Earth Am I Here For? (Rick Warren)

ABOUT THE AUTHOR

On February 1, 2011, Dr. Kent Ingle began serving as Southeastern University's fifteenth president. Before becoming SEU's president, Dr. Ingle served as the dean of the College of Ministry at Northwest University in Kirkland, Washington.

Dr. Ingle's professional ministry experience included eight years as a college professor and fifteen years of pastoral leadership to two congregations—one in Los Angeles and the other in Chicago.

Prior to entering professional ministry, Dr. Ingle spent ten years as a television sports anchor for NBC and CBS. He started as an anchor at the age of eighteen in Bakersfield, California, and finished his career in Los Angeles. He covered many professional sports teams and interviewed hundreds of notable people in the professional sports world, including Michael Jordan, Magic Johnson, Kareem Abdul-Jabbar, Pete Rose, Muhammad Ali and Carl Lewis.

Dr. Ingle earned a Bachelor of Arts degree in broadcast journalism from Vanguard University of Southern California and later completed his Master of Theological Studies at Vanguard. He received his Doctor of Ministry degree from the Assemblies of God Theological Seminary in Springfield, Missouri. He is a church coach/consultant and a conference speaker.

A California native, Dr. Ingle and his wife, Karen, reside in Lakeland, Florida, and have three teenage children: Davis, Kaila, and Paxton. The family also has two dogs, Lexi and Zoe. Dr. Ingle loves to cycle, run, lift weights, play basketball, and stay as active as possible. When he has down time, you can find him reading books on leadership or watching NBA League Pass.

To contact Dr. Kent Ingle visit www.kentingle.com

ABOUT SOUTHEASTERN UNIVERSITY

Southeastern University is a Christ-centered learning community committed to empowering students to discover and develop their divine design so they can serve Jesus and the world through spirit-empowered life, learning, and leadership. Anchored in Ephesians 2:10, Southeastern believes that every student is a masterpiece from God, created in Christ Jesus to do good works. As a result, Southeastern has designed its educational journey to prepare students to succeed professionally in order to serve God fully.

Located on a beautiful eighty-seven-acre campus in central Florida, Southeastern currently enrolls nearly 3,000 students, representing forty-seven states and forty countries. The campus is culturally diverse, operating in a variety of gifts and talents from a wide range of academic study. With more than fifty-one undergraduate degrees and thirteen graduate degrees, SEU continues to expand its influence by offering world-class education with a mission. At the heart of this vibrant community is a staff and faculty of distinction, committed to academic excellence, actively engaged in the life and development of students.

Campus life is marked by a culture of discipleship where students are challenged to excel academically, socially, and spiritually. Both in and out of the classroom, students are empowered to become lifelong learners. Through mentoring opportunities they discover their leadership capacity to live life committed to serving Christ globally. Through innovative chapel services, intramurals, and more than fifteen varsity sports, the

Southeastern "college experience" is second to none. SEU students create memories and friendships that last a lifetime.

Long after commencement, our graduates remain a part of the Southeastern community. Today, throughout the United States and around the world, Southeastern graduates are living out their divine design in positions of leadership as teachers, school administrators, journalists, attorneys, pastors, social service and mental health professionals, missionaries, musicians, and business men and women.

TO ORDER MORE COPIES OF THIS BOOK

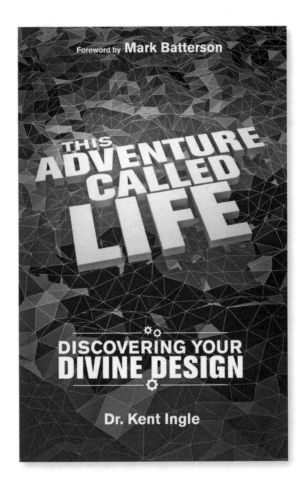